CW00820820

How To
Cycle Faster

By

Julian Bradbrook

Books in this series
by Julian Bradbrook

Table of Contents

Introduction

If you have ever seen the Tour de France competitors whizzing past in real life, or even on the television, you will have been possessed albeit briefly by the desire to get on a bike and cycle faster. Riding a bike is a childhood rite of passage for many, but for many that bike rusts away in the garage and is rarely taken out when your teens have passed. But this book hopes to help you fall in love with cycling again, and fall in love with the idea of going fast on a bike.

Of course, cycling does involve incurring some expenditure – but you can get a decent bike second hand if you keep an eye on the free ads and of course ebay. Some cycling stores sell second hand, reconditioned bikes, which can be helpful because such places typically have knowledgeable staff on hand to give plenty of advice and help. You could even hire a bike a few times, to allow you time to fall back in love with the sport without making the commitment to purchase an expensive bike.

How serious are you about cycling? This book is based on the premise that anyone, whether they cycle every day of the week or only occasionally, can learn to cycle faster. So even if you have not ridden since your teens, with a few weeks of dedicated practise, you can learn some techniques and build your cardiovascular efficiency to make you cycle more quickly.

This book will take you through the basic principles of cycling technique, and talk about the simple tweaks that you can make to improve your speed. The book will then discuss the importance of core strength – that is to say the strength in your tummy and girdle muscles. As cyclists, it is often all about the legs, but we need to consider the muscles higher up so that we harness the whole of our bodies for power. Paying attention to core strength also helps reduce the risk of injury.

We will also look at the speeds that elite athletes achieve, and also what is achievable for the rest of us mere mortals. This book is realistic and appreciates that you probably have a day job and a real life to balance with your cycling aspirations. Speaking of balance, we also look at what motivates people, and how to make yourself get on your bike when you do not really feel like it.

When the spirits are low, when the day appears dark, when work becomes monotonous, when hope hardly seems worth having, just mount a bicycle and go out for a spin down the road, without thought on anything but the ride you are taking.
Sir Arthur Conan Doyle

We will also look at how to avoid injuries and the effect of your own fuel. What you eat can have an enormous impact on how you cycle and the speed that you are capable of achieving. If you do not eat or drink the right things, you may find yourself "running out of steam".

Glossary of terms used in cycling speak

Aerobic – exercise where the body uses oxygen in the body in the process of burning fuel

Anaerobic – exercise where the body does not have time to access oxygen to use to burn fuel

Bike weights – weights that are attached to your bike in training sessions, which are designed to increase the strength of a cyclist and make the race seem easier when they have been removed.

Borg scale – Borg was a scientist who created a scale of exertion. Some sports scientists use the scale of 0 to 20, others go from 0 to 10.

Cadence – your pedal RPM. A high number of cycles per minute is a high cadence, a low number is a low cadence.

Crank power – the strength a cyclist has to crank the pedals around

Drafting – using the disturbance in the air created by the cyclist in front to your advantage

Echelon – a pace line where the cyclists in a race fall in behind each other to benefit from the slipstream that one cyclist gives another.

Fartlek – a type of speedwork that involves a variety of speeds

Hybrid – a bike that is a cross between a mountain bike and a road bike

Lactic acid – a by-product of anaerobic exercise

Masher – some who cycles with a low RPM

Peloton – the main body of cyclists in a race, who group together to save the effort of racing against aerodynamics.

Rate of perceived exertion – RPE – the athlete rates themselves on how easy or difficult they are finding the activity.

RPM – revolutions per minute – the number of times that your bike wheel goes around in a minute.

Slipstream – the wake of the cyclist in front, where the air pressure is lower

Speedwork – part of a training regime where the athlete focuses on getting faster.

Velodrome – specially designed cycling track for high speed riding where the sides are banked

VO2 max – the efficiency with which your body uses oxygen in the system.

Chapter 1 - Targets for speed cycling – what is fast?

There are a variety of distances that you can cycle over, so if you are new to cycling, you could try a number of courses.

Sprinting

For men and women sprint world records are divided into those with a standing start, and those with a flying start (and if you were wondering where the expression came from – this is it).

Flying starts time trials are those that measure the cyclist's progress as they go between fixed points, having had a "run up" to the first point.

For men, the 200m flying time trial record is 9.572 and is held by Sireau from France.

For women, the 200m flying time trial record is held by German Welte at 10.642.

For 500m, the men's record is help by Chris Hoy at 24.758, and for women, Russian Salumae at 29.635.

Amateur cyclists typically do not have the chance to try out these kinds of sprints, and do not have the equipment for accurate time trials. However, if you are lucky enough to live near a velodrome that has an open day, you should go along and give it a try!

Pursuits

In a pursuit race, the athletes start at opposite ends of the track, and then try to catch the other one. If one catches the other, a victory is declared. But if no one gets caught, the cyclist with the best time wins.

The hour record

This is a strange kind of a race, where the cyclist rides as far as they possibly can in 1 hour. Some commentators report that athletes typically attempt this at the end of their career, although it is fun to try at any stage.

For record breaking attempts, professional cyclists make their attempts in velodromes, which are not seen as equal – the one in Milan is apparently the fastest track in the world.

The men's record for the one hour ride is a distance of 56.375 km. For women, the record is 46.065km. Of course, to ride as hard as you can is dangerous on an open road. Nevertheless, if you ride safely in a quiet area, it can be fun to try with friends to see how far you can go within the magic hour. Depending on the terrain, you should be able to get several kilometres under your belt. This is a good exercise to repeat from time to time, as with the benefit of speedwork your one hour distance should eventually increase over a few months.

Stage races

These are races that are spread out over a number
of different stages. The winner is the person with
the lowest time added up. So you do not have to
win each "leg" to win overall – you may have a
blazingly fast race that makes up for not being the
quickest in the other parts of the race. These are
interesting to keep track of, and can last several
days. The Tour de France is an example of a staged
race, as the athletes stop at night and travel down
to the next start line. With the Tour de France,
entry is only possible by invitation from the
organisers. It takes place over three weeks in July,
and the person who leads at the beginning of each
stage gets to wear the yellow jersey which signifies
their position.

Ultra marathons

Even the name of these races sounds intimidating.
There is no set length for a race to constitute an
ultra marathon. One of the most famous is the race
that takes competitors from one American coast to
the other, called the Race Across America. The
cyclists can cycle for days, and must take at least
40 hours of rest during the course, which is then
deducted from their time. Unlike stage races,
which take place at civilised times in the day, the
Race Across America expects cyclists to travel
through the night, as they fight to get the fastest
time. The route is typically similar every year
(unlike the Tour de France), and cyclists cover

approximately 3,000 miles in around 8 or 9 days. Realistically, this is not a race for amateurs. There are strict qualifying conditions (based on your previous performance in other events) and the drop-out rate, even for people who have met these strict criteria, is 1 in 2.

The need for a vehicle with flashing lights following at night and a medical and supplies team means that only those cyclists who have sponsorship or deep pockets can compete.

What about the rest of us?

If a velodrome is a while away and the Tour de France and the Race Across America might as well be on a different planet, how can the rest of us measure our cycling speed, and determine what is respectable and what is embarrassing? To put this into perspective, amateur cyclists typically burn between 250 and 400 calories on a 3 hour run. During a similar length of time, your Tour de France rider burns between 4,000 and 5,000 calories.

So what speeds can you hope to achieve? With monitors being affordable and widely available, it is simple to measure your velocity. Beginners could hope to cycle at 10mph on flat terrain. This is also what relatively fit cyclists would achieve on uphill stretches. On the flat, people who put the hours into their fitness and speedwork can realistically achieve 17 mph with some dedication. On a downhill stretch on a well tarmacked road, you could hope for 35mph. some amateur cyclists report that they believe they could probably go faster, but that they are afraid to do so for fear of coming off the bike. There is some sense in this! Mountain descents completed by professionals can clock in at up to 65mph, but these are people with first aid teams on standby, who do this day in and day out and stake their professional reputation on the speed that they reach. The weekend cyclist does not have the luxury of a road that is closed to traffic and a safety crew on hand.

Chapter 2 - Focus on technique

When you learn to ride a bike, it feels amazing to be able to balance yourself upright, propel yourself forward, and steer in the right direction. Once you have learnt how to do that, it is unusual to revisit the issue of technique. Riding a bike is considered to be something that you can either do or you can't.

However, when you start to think about adjusting your technique to increase your speed, you may wish to consider how you can tinker with stroke to get the most out of your strong legs. There are many different methods of improving your technique, and we will begin with increasing cranking power, then talk about improving your pedal stroke efficiency and then look at your RPM (revolutions per minute). By looking at these issues in turn and working at them in a few dedicated training sessions, any cyclist should be able to increase their speed.

Cranking power

When cyclists discuss the best way to increase their cranking power, they often say that the best way to do this is to cycle more. This is on the basis that improved endurance will be result from cycling efforts. The further you go, the theory goes, the stronger you get and the more powerful your legs become. In fact, some cyclists believe that simply cycling as long and as hard as you can is the best way to become a better cyclist.

Is this true? Yes and no. Your endurance will improve, as will your strength, but you will simply repeat mistakes in your technique that you have developed, again and again, and not have learned anything new.

Even just a couple of sessions of training to improve your cranking power will pay volumes when you hit those longer rides again. So start by setting aside a training session specifically for developing your cranking power.

Starting your cranking power workout

The first thing to consider is where you should practise your cycling technique. The ideal place is a long stretch of road or track, without much of a gradient. Slight ascents and descents are fine, but this is not a hill training exercise, so steep hills should be avoided. Training outside is the preferred option (over using a stationary bike), because it is the environment most similar to the one in which you race. But if you are unlikely to train in bad weather, or if you find yourself near the gym in your lunch break, using a stationary bike is better than not doing your cranking power training at all.

You will never find the "perfect" trail, no matter how hard you look for it. So if you find a piece of road that is just about good enough, go for it.

As with any training exercise, whichever training environment you choose, you must warm up adequately, to prepare your muscles and joints for the exercise ahead.

To begin with, start off in a low gear for around a minute or two. Next, alternate thirty seconds of low gear cycling with thirty seconds of high gear cycling, so that your body feels alternately challenged and relaxed. You only need to do five sets of these alternate thirty second segments before you are ready for the main workout.

Stepping things up

The next step is to up your exertion levels. Athletes of all disciplines often use a Borg scale (named after the sports physiologist who devised it) to rate their level of perceived exertion. There are a number of different ways of doing this, but a 0-10 scale is typical.

Using this scale, 0 would be doing nothing, and 10 would be pushing yourself so hard that you are near to breaking point. Exercising for too long at 10 would be a shortcut to burnout. Realistically, 10 on these scales is intended to be a theoretical point of reference. No coach would advise actually reaching this level.

For the purpose of this cranking power exercise, the warm up stage mentioned above where you are using the lowest gear would be around 1. Your body is comfortable with this, and there is virtually no challenge whatsoever.

But to increase your cranking power, go up to level 7 or 8 for thirty seconds, by using a much higher gear than you would typically use for that terrain and speed. You may find that the number of revolutions per minute drop at this point, but that is nothing to worry about in the early stages, as your body is just adapting to the higher resistance. The next stage of the exercise is to take it back down to level 1 or so, by changing down again to a much lower gear for around ninety seconds to let your body recover.

Then you can go up again to level 7 or 8 for another thirty seconds, and so on.

The point of this exercise is to make your body not only stronger, but also more responsive. To keep switching after thirty and then ninety seconds means that your nervous system must act quickly to make sure that you are doing the right thing at the right time.

When you first start including cranking power workouts into your training regime, the central part of the workout should not be continued for longer than 20 minutes. But as it becomes a more regular part of your training, it can be sustained for up to 30 minutes.

Cooling things down

When you have done between twenty and thirty minutes of the cranking power exercise, you need to cool down, to allow your heart rate to recover.

Start to cool down by making the low gear section of your workout last for one minute at a time, instead of 30 seconds. And then reduce the gear of the "high gear" section by one gear each time, until you are riding normally.

The aim of this cool down is to bring you back to an even rate of cycling, and also to bring your heart rate down gradually. Cooling down properly is essential to reduce the risk of injury.

How can you measure improvement in your cranking power?

This is a difficult question, because what cycling "feels" like can vary so much from cyclist to cyclist. However, after just a couple of cranking power technique sessions, you should find that your legs become stronger and cycling in the middle gears becomes easier.

Pedal stroke efficiency

What is pedal stroke efficiency? It is a term that cyclists use to describe how to get the maximum amount of power out of the action of turning a pedal in a circle, while expending the minimum amount of energy. It stands to reason that the less energy you expend, the longer you can continue cycling. Accordingly, pedal stroke efficiency is helpful for endurance races.

What seems to be a simple activity (making the pedal go around) can actually be broken down into four "zones", which will be discussed below and roughly correspond with quarters, or times on a clock.

By paying attention to the exact position of the pedal and the level of exertion that is required in each zone and realigning them as necessary, you can squeeze out more power with less effort.

Starting pedal stroke efficiency training

Before you begin, have you considered your hip-knee-ankle alignment? This is where it can help to train with someone else, as it is sometimes difficult to judge whether or not you are vertically aligned. When your training partner looks at you head on, your hip, knee and ankle should be in a line at all zones of the pedal stroke. The most common offender to be out of alignment is your knee, which it can be tempting to push out as your progress through the zones. A common theme in this book is that alignment is the secret to injury avoidance, and to efficiency.

Given that most mobile phones can take moving pictures, get your training partner to record you cycling for a few strokes. You may be surprised to see how misaligned you are, even when you felt that you were cycling straight. For some people, the first time they notice their misalignment is a photo from a set of race pictures.

When you first alter your alignment to straighten up, you may initially feel knee pain. This is because you are trying to change the habits of years of training. Whatever you were doing initially suited your current muscle set-up, so you must expect some kind of resistance from your body to the change.

However, if pain persists beyond a couple of training rides, consult a sports physiologist, as you may have a biomechanical imbalance that needs specialist medical attention.

The next thing to consider is the position of your saddle. You need to consider both the height of the saddle, but also the fore-aft position. Is the saddle tipping you forward, or encouraging you to lean too far back?

If your saddle is too low, you will end up bending your knees more than necessary, which is a fast track to chronic knee pain. On the other hand, if your saddle is too high, you will not have given yourself the flexibility you need to adjust your ankle position throughout all of the zones. A perfectly positioned saddle should mean that your knee should be only ever so slightly bent when your pedal is at 6 o'clock.

The zones of a pedal stroke

Before you even start any pedal stroke efficiency training, look at how you currently cycle. Mentally mark out 12, 3, 6 and 9 o'clock in your current style, and think about the angle of your foot at these times. Which muscles feel tense, and which relaxed? Where are you knees in these zones? Are they sticking out? Once again, this is where a moving picture of yourself can teach you volumes.

Now that you feel aware of what happens when throughout the zones, consider taking them one by one and adjusting your technique for maximum efficiency.

Zone 1

True zone 1 carries on from 12 o'clock to 5 o'clock (and does not stop at 3 o'clock), and is where the cyclist experiences the most intense period of muscle exertion. This is the biggest part of the downstroke, and is where you need to enlist the large muscles in your upper legs as your foot comes down. The secret here is dropping your heel as soon as possible in zone 1, so that your feet are parallel to the ground as you go past 3 o'clock. Just doing this alone will considerably improve your pedal stroke efficiency, and in fact some coaches believe that stopping here in pedal stroke training can significantly advance your speed. But why stop here when you have 3 other zones to improve on?

Zone 2

If zone 1 is about dropping your heel, zone 2 is about pointing your toes, for which of course strong ankles are essential. As your foot travels around from 3o'clock to 6 o'clock, you should end up with your toe pointing down by about 20 degrees. Some cyclists say that this should look and feel as though you are scraping something unpleasant off the bottom of your shoe! To develop and get better at this toe pointing stage, perform some ankle strengthening exercises. It may help to say to yourself "point" between 3 o'clock and 6 o'clock while you are riding along for a couple of hundred metres, to embed this as a habit.

Zone 3

What exactly is happening in zone 3? The general effort felt in your legs while cycling may lead you to believe that you are pulling your foot up. However, what is really happening is that their legs are being pushed up by the pedal. The key here is to make sure that you are not losing any more power than you have to on zone 3, by making sure that your legs are strong enough to keep you in control of the bike, rather than the other way around.

Zone 4

It would be easy to assume that zone 4 is a passive phase, where the cyclist waits for the pedal to push her foot up and anticipates starting the downward stroke in zone 1 again. But this is not the case. By pushing your knee forward in this zone, you can be ahead of the curve and go into zone 1 with some momentum already going.

RPM

Like any other method of travelling which involves wheels, cycling is faster when you have a high number of RPM (revolutions per minute). The interplay between RPM and the gear you use

determines the speed a cyclist is capable of.
Cyclists are also concerned about their efficiency.
So what is the ideal RPM for a cyclist, or is there
no such thing?

As usual, this is a hot topic among cyclists, which
many different views around. Some people believe
that the higher the RPM the better, whilst others
think that if you are cycling a long way, a more
modest RPM is easier to sustain and does not wear
you out as quickly.

Looking at the evidence out there, it seems that
pedalling at between 80rpm and 85 rpm is the most
efficient way of cycling, whether the cyclist is
travelling over flat ground, steep inclines or
lumpier terrain. Lance Armstrong has made high
cadence cycling popular, by including dashes of
over 90 rpm regularly in his winning sprints.
Amateur cyclists have imitated this practice,
without really understanding why their
performance has improved.

Now in a recent trial, scientists at the Universities
of Wisconsin and Wyoming have conducted
research that has worked out why this is RPM is
the best.

After extensive testing, the joint study revealed
that the way in which glycogen is used up in slow
and fast pedalling is different. During slow
pedalling, fast twitch muscles lost their glycogen
very quickly, but during the fast pedalling, the
slow twitch muscles were able to regulate
glycogen consumption much better. Glycogen is

the way in which energy is stored in muscles, and cannot be restored as quickly as it is used up, so it is important to exercise in such a way that it is used as efficiently as possible.

For the purposes of this study, the scientists asked cyclists to cycle for two sessions of 30 minutes each. In both sessions, the cyclists worked at 85% of their VO2 max. VO2 max is a measure of someone's maximum aerobic capacity – their ability to transport oxygen around their body. Generally this can be increased by training and improving your cardiovascular stamina. However, your VO2 max is also something that is affected by your genetic inheritance. Some top athletes are naturally blessed with an amazing capacity to use oxygen efficiently, while others may have to work that little bit harder thanks to a lower VO2 max.

So whilst the cyclists in this study each worked at 85% of their VO2 max, for one of those sessions they pedalled at 50 rpm in a high gear. In the other session, they pedalled at 100rpm in a low gear. In both 30min sessions, they travelled the same distance at identical speeds.

When the scientists measured the oxygen consumption of the cyclists, they found that the two sessions were the same. There was no significant difference in heart rates, or blood lactate levels, or oxygen consumption levels. But there was a significant difference in how quickly the cyclists broke down the carbohydrate in their muscles (which is stored as glycogen).

Uniformly across all the cyclists in the study, in the 50rpm sessions the energy they used came from their muscles, whereas at 100rpm, energy came far more from fat.

There was a difference in how fast twitch and slow twitch muscles behaved, because the fast twitch ones lost 50% of glycogen at 50rpm, compared with just 33% from their slow twitch counterparts. The results of the study therefore prove that fast pedalling is more efficient (and, as it happens, the best way to burn fat if losing weight is a priority of yours).

However, there is a point at which a high rpm is too fast for your body to cope with, and can be counter effective. For instance, if you are pedalling at over 110 rpm, you will find that the momentum of the wheel is doing more than your leg muscles. The wheel is turning your leg, rather than the other way around. In this situation, you can run the risk of injury if you lose control.

As the rpm increases, so does the danger of injury. Finally, given that momentum pretty much takes over at 200rpm, you also lose cardiovascular benefits of cycling – after all it is the bike and not your muscles that are making the wheels go around. So it does not follow that the fat burning power of cycling at 200rpm is double that of 100 rpm – rather the reverse.

If you are a triathlete, there is another consideration to bear in mind. Some triathletes claim that it is best to keep a similar cadence for your cycling and running, so that it is "easier" (if indeed any variation of the word easy can be used in the context of triathletes!) to switch between the two. Anything above 90 rpm makes the transition from cycling to running or vice versa feel too strange, as rpm above that level cannot be upheld in running.

Are you a masher or a spinner?

Until you take your cycling seriously and consider the question, you might be surprised at how fast or slow you pedal. In fact, you probably have never considered the issue.

But when it comes to rpm, training coaches divide cyclists into two different groups – mashers – who have low rpm at high gears, and spinners – who have high rpm in low gears.

Mashers make the most use of fast twitch muscle fibres, whereas spinners make more use of slow twitch muscle fibres, which do not consume as much oxygen or produce as much glycogen as fast twitch muscle fibres.

Finding the best rpm for you is matter of trial and error. The "ideal" rpm for you will depend on your body shape, your fitness, and which kind of bike you like to ride. It stands to reason that a couch potato will be less comfortable at a high rpm than a whippet.

How do you increase cadence (rpm)?

Naturally, after learning more about the effects of rpm, you may want to look at increasing your cadence, especially if like most beginner cyclists you are currently riding at around 60 rpm.

Spinning classes will help this, but you can also use a monitor on your bike and train while paying specific attention to it.

If you are planning a regime to up your rpm over time, you should only try to increase your cadence by 5rpm per week, as gradual changes to the way you train are typically much better for your body.

What is low cadence work good for?

If high cadence cycling is generally the most efficient, it does not follow that low cadence cycling is waste of time, or that it has no place in your training regime.

In fact, low cadence runs can be built into your speedwork. Changing the intensity of your pedal stroke can be part of the variation that you need to develop your overall speed. Low cadence can also be useful for building up muscle mass.

Chapter 3 - What does speedwork mean for cyclists?

When you say "speedwork", you may think immediately of runners. This may be because you might take note of more runners rather than cyclists doing dedicated speedwork on the road. But cyclists can also benefit from setting aside specific portions of their training time to travelling faster.

For those who tend to take part in long events, speedwork can feel like a diversion from their ordinary training regime. It can feel like playing at training. However, when you have got a few speedwork sessions under your belt, you will notice a considerable improvement in your performance.

What kinds of speedwork can cyclists do?

Interval training

Intervals involve cyclists travelling for certain distances at varying speeds. Typically a cyclist will travel 500m or 1km at full pelt, and then perform a slower 500m or 1km, and then a faster one, and so on.

How can you do this if you do not know the exact measurements of your trail? If you are a road cyclist, the answer is to drive it first and mentally mark out the route as you drive past particular road marks. Interval training does not have to be an exact science. The point of it is that the intervals should be roughly regular, and that you should be consistent when you return to the activity again. You can of course spend some time on a cycling track, but if you want to avoid the formality of this, if you do not have one nearby or if you do not feel confident to show up with your old and unfashionable bike at a cycling destination, it is still possible to do interval training in the "real world" and get good results.

It can be useful to do your interval training with a partner, especially if you are a reluctant speedwork cyclist. Using a training partner can help to keep you on the case, and measure your results for you. If the route allows, you could even race against each other.

Done properly, interval training is hard on cyclists, and for that reason should not be attempted until you have been training seriously for at least 8 weeks. As a proportion of your training schedule, intervals should not make up more than one fifth.

Fartlek training

"Fartlek" is Swedish for speed play, and by the nature of its name cyclists can tell that it is nothing to be afraid of. You may in fact already include some fartlek in your current training regime, without really knowing it.

By varying your speed for certain distances, you can develop techniques that improve your speed overall. For example, you may wish to cycle as

fast as you can to a certain landmark, then slow
down to the next, then pick up the pace, then cycle
at maximum power and so on.

The point about fartlek is that it is informal: you
play with your pace and see how it turns out.
When you are cycling, fartlek can be fun to do
with a training partner, as you can race each other
on the fast bursts. As long as you include enough
slow cycling at the beginning, you can include
fartlek in your warm up to give you an interesting
lead in to your cycling routine.

Fartlek can be practised whatever level of fitness
you have. Newcomers to the sport can get
something out of this, in the same way that people
who have been cycling for years can benefit from
speed play.

To a certain extent, the results do not have to be
measured. The point is that you vary your pace,
and the effort that you put in to get to different
landmarks.

A measured route

Cyclists can be forgiven for wondering what the
point of speedwork is, if they do not feel any
immediate benefit. The answer to this is to find a
route or trail that is easily available to you, and to
ride it every two months or so to track your
progress. If you notice a significant improvement
in your time, you can assume that the speedwork
has been a success.

On the other hand, if you are not seeing any real progress, ask yourself whether you are truly working hard enough in your training. Do you push yourself in your fartlek training, or is there too much fun and not enough speed? Are your intervals long enough in your interval training to get enough speed up? By tweaking your speedwork, you could make considerable progress when you decide to do your next time trial.

Chapter 4 - Endurance, stamina and muscle fatigue

When you first start cycling, the idea of cycling for 100km (a "century") seems about as realistic as cycling for a million miles. How can people possibly manage a hundred kilometres, when you can barely manage fifteen? And how can they manage to cover that distance at some considerable speed?

It is important to remember at this point that even winners of the Tour de France and the Race Across America had to start somewhere.

This chapter deals with specific techniques that you can use to build up your cycling endurance. Building endurance is necessary before you build your speed.

One step (or one wheel) at a time

Nobody starts out on a 100km ride in their first week of cycling. Or even their first month, or quarter. But the trick to building up to this length of ride is that the build-up has to be slow and gradual, so that before you realise it you can cycle for 25km without feeling as though your legs are on fire the next day.

If you have ever tried to build your endurance at running, you will be relieved to learn that you can add kilometres to your maximum cycle distance much, much more quickly than you can with running. That is because your cycling stamina is not related so much to the ability of your body and your joints to withstand the pounding of the pavements that is necessary to succeed in extending your running capacity. So you can add the kilometres without adding too much pressure to your joints.

However, you should not be tempted to add too many kilometres too quickly, because an upsurge in training too soon in your cycling career can put you at risk of injury, and can perhaps put you at risk of becoming disheartened if you feel you have failed at something too soon. Far better to give yourself easy wins by adding a couple of kilometres at a time.

Cross train to avoid injury and boost endurance

If you are the type of person who finds doing the same thing day in day out boring, then you will be relieved to hear that cross training could be the answer to extending your cycling endurance and building your stamina.

If you have already spent a fortune on an expensive racing bike, you will be glad to hear that you do not need to join a costly gym to be able to get your fix of cross training! Why not don a pair of running shoes and get a great cardiovascular workout by stepping outside of your door and seeing where the mood takes you? Running can be great for getting a quick burst of cardiovascular activity. A 30 minute run can be the perfect answer if you want some exercise but do not have time to go for a decent length ride.

Other cross training activities that can be of use for boosting cycling endurance include swimming, where the resistance of the water provides a low impact push for you. There is hardly any pressure on your joints, so you can swim for at least 30 minutes even when you are rehabilitating an injury that prevents you from cycling. A further benefit of swimming is that is arms led, rather than the leg led activities of cycling and running.

Thinking of even more gentle pursuits that can boost endurance, have you considered Pilates and yoga? Both can boost core strength and posture – helpful for someone whose chosen sport sees them slouched over handlebars for hours each week.

Add variety into your training week

Cycling the same route every week is great way to measure your progress. What seemed like torture at the beginning of your cycling career can now seem easy. But sticking to the same routes all the time can make you bored and lose motivation. Try to add a bit of variety. If you can, add some hill training into your training, although do not be tempted off road if you do not have the appropriate bike or tyres. Hill training can be gradual to begin with, and will still make a difference.

Introducing gradients here and there can increase your stamina no end, and make you desperate to get back to your old "boring" routine!

If you do not have much choice available in the routes available, why not change the distances that you cycle to add some variety. Sometimes a fast 5km can be more challenging than a steady 20km, and certainly makes the same streets around you seem a little more interesting.

Make your rides long and steady

Some cyclists claim that riding low and slow can boost their endurance. However, this method ultimately leads to frustration, as the cyclist does not become any faster – instead he sees hours of his life disappear on slow rides!

By riding long and steady- i.e. not burning yourself out with distances that are too far or speeds that are unsustainable, a cyclist can boost his endurance gradually but measurably over a number of weeks. You should also be gradually increasing your speed.

Cyclists who push the "long and slow" method may ultimately be people who are perplexed as to why they are overweight, notwithstanding all the cycling they do. But the answer is that the long and slow method simply does not burn enough calories to have much of an effect on weight. At the same time, the cyclist has developed a mental image of himself as someone who does hours of exercise, and considers himself to have earned the right to eat what he wants with no consequence.

Leave plenty of time for recovery

It is easy to think that the bike, not the cyclist takes the strain, so there is not much need for recovery. However, cyclists who do not leave enough time in their schedule for recover leave themselves open to burn out, which is the beginning of the end for any athlete. Lack of recovery time can also cause boredom.

By leaving yourself enough time to recover between long rides, you give your body the chance to repair any damage caused by overuse of certain parts of the legs, and you also give your muscles the chance to rebuild their depleted glycogen reserves.

Certain warning signs mean that your body is urging you to take a rest day or two, and should be heeded immediately. These include:

- a fast resting heart rate (unusual for very fit people);
- feeling run down and being susceptible to colds and the flu;
- dark urine; and
- a feeling of all over soreness that will not go away.

Don't forget speedwork

What part does speedwork play in a cyclist's quest for endurance? Unlike runners, cyclists do not have to choose between speed and distance. It is true that professional cyclists do engage in 200m and 500m sprints, but the typical (albeit serious) cyclist will ride for at least 5km at a time, so speed and distance are inseparable.

The short bursts of intense energy needed in fast intervals and the sprint parts of fartlek provide quick moments of anaerobic activity, which, if regularly included in your training regime mean that your body will become more efficient at processing the lactic acid that is involved with producing it. There is an element of "treat 'em mean to keep 'em keen" here, as your body simply becomes used to disposing of the stuff.

Likewise, speedwork sharpens your central nervous system, which means that your muscles' ability to move when you want them to will be heightened.

Using bike weights

Weights on your bike, are you mad? Bike weights divide opinion among regular cyclists. Some find that after training with weights, races become easier when the weights are removed. The reduction in the power needed to travel the same distance gives the cyclist a new lease of life, which for some people acts as a turbo booster in a race situation. They suddenly feel lighter, and therefore more confident of a better time, which is a self-fulfilling prophecy as they go on to achieve what they now believe they are capable of.

Other cyclists find them too disorienting. They know the feel of their own weight and their bike weight so well that to tinker with it throws them off kilter.

Why not try some for a couple of training sessions to see which camp you fall into?

Chapter 5 - Speed tips for road cycling

Using other cyclists – drafting

The holy grail in cycling fast is the preservation of energy. Given that you are likely to be cycling for hours rather than just minutes, conserving as much energy as possible and deploying what you have as efficiently as you can is important.

One of the most effective things that a cyclist can do is to make use of the low pressure area that is created behind the person in front of them. This is why you see a group of riders cycling together in road races. The pack is technically known as the peloton, and the behaviour of those cyclists and the way in which they interact can have as much effect on overall speeds and outcomes of the race as their cyclists' talent and strength.

Why does drafting work?

As a matter of simple physics, when a cyclist moves forward she creates vortices of wind in her wake (this is easy to visualise if you think about a boat creating its own wake in the water behind it. The water looks as though it has been "chopped up"). This disturbed air is of lower pressure than the general atmospheric pressure felt on a lone cyclist as they are moving forward. So the low pressure air in the wake of the cyclist in front means that you can move forward through it with less wind resistance. Some scientists believe that you can conserve up to 40% of your energy by riding in someone else's slip stream.

This set-up is also advantageous to the rider in front, who experiences a slight feeling of propulsion from the cyclist following her taking up some of the low pressure wake zone. However, she has to expend more energy than her follower to make the same progress.

Between the two of them, they expend considerably less energy than two lone cyclists would put together.

Newcomers to the sport may think that this information is only relevant to professional, elite athletes, but the physics works no matter what level you are at. It is worthwhile trying to put this into practise even as a cycling newbie.

Top drafting techniques to follow
By following these tips, you can use drafting techniques like a pro.

- Get as close as possible to the person in front. This of course depends on the conditions. If the road is slippery due to excess rain, then this is not really practical. However, the closer you get to the cyclist ahead of you, the greater the aerodynamic benefits are that you can reap. If you typically ride 18 inches behind your leader, try closing that gap up to 12 inches. If you are riding at a gap of 12 inches, try closing that gap to 6 inches, assuming that you are skilled enough to do that safely and that the leader is also skilled enough. You should also consider where you are in the peloton, as the further down the line you are, the more aerodynamic benefits you can reap from the arrangement.

- If a peloton is a pack, then an echelon is a line, typically falling diagonally across the road where the race is taking place. You are unlikely to have the confidence or skill to join an echelon on your first ever road race, but observe the other cyclists carefully and watch how they are managing to keep just the right amount of space between each other. An echelon is formed by racing cyclists in response to a crosswind that blows across the road. As with a peloton, the leaders face the brunt of the aerodynamic resistance, and those behind benefit from their slipstream and from being sheltered from the wind itself.

Funnily enough, there is often a battle for the places at the end of an echelon (as opposed to the start), because during a long race this is where you are likely to save the most energy. Cycling courtesy dictates that cyclists take their turn in the various positions in the peloton and in the echelon, so that the beneficial effects of the formations are shared out among the competitors. If you do not joint an echelon when it is being formed, the chances are that it will pull ahead of you and you will have to chase it to catch up.

- Be aware of the wind direction. This should really go without saying in a sport whose biggest enemy is aerodynamics. But cyclists ignore the wind at their peril, and then wonder why they are not making any progress against it. In particular, you should make a mental note of the wind direction before you mount an advance up the pack. Having the protection of the peloton makes it much less strenuous to ease yourself forward than fighting a cross wind.

- Avoid braking where you can. Braking destroys and negates the effort that you used to build up your speed in the first place. So when you break, you have to start again from scratch when it is time to accelerate. If you are used to watching other riders, you will soon be able to tell who the slower ones are, and who is prone to sharp decelerations. If you do need to slow down, the smart way to do this is to use aerodynamics to your own advantage. Slow down by sitting up, to offer a more resistant profile to the wind. Then resume your normal cycling position when you are ready to accelerate again.

- Go as quickly as you can around corners, where it is safe to do so.
- React quickly to changes in speed of the rider in front of you. It can be tempting to wait to see what she does, and simply follow. But try instead to anticipate what she will do next so that you end up accelerating at the same time, and enjoy the maximum benefits of her slipstream. Do exercise caution here though, because getting this wrong could jeopardise everyone else in the pace line.
- Make sure that you keep your speed as constant as possible during the race. The pack should be doing this too, and it is important to be able to keep up with them, no matter what the road throws at you. It is much easier to mount a sprint challenge at the end of a long race where you have kept up a constant, respectable speed, rather than when you have exhausted yourself with the burst and retreats.
- Have you heard of the accordion effect? This is where small adjustments in speed at the font of the pace line or peloton can lead, in the style of Chinese whispers, to a distorted lot of heavy braking near the back of the race. For that reason, it is advisable to stay near the front.

- Make sure that you have included a number of aerodynamic positions in your training. For instance, if you tend to have a "sit up and beg" stance when you are cycling, then dropping your head as soon as you get into the peloton will feel weird and unnatural, and will not be the position that you are used to training in. Make sure that your body is versatile enough to cope with cycling in a variety of positions, so that you can adapt easily to different positions in the echelon.

The sprint for the finish

The sprint finish is the most important part of a cycling race, for the cyclist and for the people watching! On one hand, a cyclist's ability to sprint is informed by how much fast twitch muscle fibre they have at their disposal. The balance between fast and slow twitch fibres is genetically set – but you can change the effectiveness of those muscles. How can you improve your sprinting technique? As with everything else to do with cycling, improvements can really only be made with practise. This is where speedwork comes in – particularly interval training. Including 30 second sprints in your speedwork bring a bit of adrenalin to your training sessions, and can be fun too. Due to its intensity, sprinting is anaerobic, as energy is burned in the muscles so quickly that the process happens before your blood can get enough oxygen to them.

Further training tips for road cyclists

- No matter how limited the amount of time you have available per week, do not forget warm up and cool downs as part of your regime. These are not parts of the training schedule that can be cut out. They are essential to becoming a better athlete.

- If you can possibly afford it, hire a training coach, even if it is only for a period of six weeks to give your training a boost.

- Keep a log, but this will be useless if you never look at it. Be your own strictest critic, and be honest about the effort that you have put in. On the sprinting part of your interval training, did you have anything left in the tank? Did you set aside all the hours that you could this week for road race training? Have you rested enough? Are you eating healthily enough? It is important to pull all of your efforts together to get the best road race performance.

Chapter 6 - Speed tips for mountain biking

What you need when you are mountain biking more than anything else is the power to get you across the challenging terrain. Without strength, you will not be going anywhere.

If you are new to mountain biking and have decided to leave the road for a while for more challenging terrain, it might be so different that you wonder whether this is the same sport! Suddenly, where aerodynamics had ruled, strength has taken over. Instead of leaning forward and focusing on the back side of the cyclist in front, you find yourself sitting up and taking notice of what is around you. And with mountain bike racing, what is around you might be of much more interest than the back side of the cyclist in front. Mountain bikers also need to know the territory well, or at least have had a good study of the map before the event. In a sense, mountain biking is more interesting than road racing because it involves exploring new territories, although of course there can be a risk that mountain bikers who are new to the area where the race is being held may get distracted by the views!

Most of all, mountain bikers need stamina, to keep going in adverse conditions. This can be an issue when the going under foot (or under wheel, as is more appropriate) is so challenging that you do not make much progress forward. But you need to remember that in some races the point is that not everyone will finish, let alone that not everyone will finish fast. A tough mental attitude is essential where there are no crowds to cheer you on.

Quick speed tips

If you are brand new to cycling of any kind, or if you are a recent convert from road racing, specific speed tips for mountain biking could include:

- Make sure that your equipment is suitable for off-roading. Taking your road bike off road is a recipe for injury, breaking down and quite frankly embarrassment! What is more, your road bike probably cost a fortune, so should not be treated as a rough and ready mountain bike. If you cannot commit to either road biking or mountain biking, why not try a hybrid bike and get two sets of tyres that you change according to the terrain;

- If at all possible, ride the course before the actual race so that you know every rock, puddle and steep incline;

- Follow a leader, but more for the psychological benefits of pacing yourself against someone rather than for slipstream (although there may be a tiny slipstream advantage here). Do not get as hung up on the echelon or peloton, if they exist. You should spent more time and energy worrying about where your wheels are going;

- If you do not know the course, do not count on a sprint finish, as the terrain may make this impossible;
- Make sure that your bike is as light as it can be. In mountain biking as in road cycling weight is everything, but you must never compromise on strength;
- Carry the equipment that you need to conduct basic repairs to your own bike, because it is more likely to break down off road. This is more important than it is with road biking, because the locations of trails are more remote – there is less chance of anyone being able to reach you quickly to help you;
- Do not enter a race that is considerably longer than your practice rides. You may think that you can add 10km to your distance, but 10km of extra hill terrain is very different from 10km of extra paved road;
- Pace yourself well. Attack hills with quiet determination rather than fury, so that you do not run out of steam. Remember that with every painful ascent, there is a fun and satisfying descent at the other side waiting for you!;

- Be realistic. With some races, simply being able to finish on challenging terrain is an achievement in itself.
- Do not shy away from bobbly tyres. Road racers used to slick road tyres may be horrified when they look at the chubby tyres used with mountain bikes, but they are like that for a reason – to provide stability and traction. Do not be tempted to substitute them for slicks as you may find yourself going nowhere rather than going fast;
- Have fun on the way down hills, but do not go mad on steep descents. If you find the uphill sections frustrating, you still have to bear in mind safety when it comes to the downhill stretches. The consequences of coming off down a mountain path are much more severe than the consequences of coming off on a road.
- Pay attention to your cadence (pedal RPM). This, more than anything else if your ticket to going faster off road. If you can get your cadence up as you cross tough terrain, you can compete with the best of them;
- If your training has been conducted mostly or almost exclusively on the road, be realistic about the speeds that you are likely to achieve.

Chapter 7 - The importance of core strength

Why is core strength so important?

Do you have legs that pray for the summer to come around, so you can get into some shorts and show them off? Are your legs strong and powerful looking, with muscles so defined you can see them through cycling shorts? And does your stomach look at disappointing by comparison?

Many cyclists are disappointed that they continue to carry weight around their middle, when they do hours of exercise a week and believe that they are burning hundreds of calories. Unfortunately, this is just a symptom of modern life, given that you probably drive to work, drive to pick the kids up from school, and in your chosen hobby sit down and cycle!

If you have noticed that you develop a lower back ache as races progress, and that you slow when you go around corners, and that your tummy seems to hurt before your legs do in long endurance races, you need to work on strengthening your core.

When you ride, your weight is supported by your handlebar, saddle and pedals. Accordingly, this tripod position takes all of the strain, but takes your core strength for granted, without doing anything to build it up. So whilst cycling is an intense workout for the legs themselves, the core is called upon, but not developed.

It is possible to introduce moves into your rides that can help to stretch your core muscles, like resting your hands gently on your handlebars and gently arching and flexing your back. However, to build strength rather than stretch, it is necessary to do some exercises like the ones listed below.

Which muscles do you need to work?

The short answer is – all of them! The core muscles should work together as a unit, which is why they are often described as a "girdle".

Muscles worked in the core exercises set out below include:

- Transverse abdominus (the one on the very inside);
- Glutes;
- Hamstrings;
- Obliques;
- Hip flexors

Core exercises to try to strengthen your gut before your next race

The exercises set out below will not take long to try out. Given that the plan here is to make your abdominal muscles work together, you should really try to do all of them in one session. It is natural that you will find one side of your body is stronger than the other (i.e. front or back).

However, by doing all of the exercises, you can build up a core strength that is universal.

Oval crunch

This exercise sounds like a breakfast cereal for children, but in fact it is a way of working the lower back, obliques and transverse abdominus, and acknowledges that the body moves in a fluid way when you are cycling.

Lie on your back, on an exercise mat with your hands behind your head. Without using your hands to pull up your head, lift your head, neck and lower back off the mat gently. Then move the area that you have lifted off the mat in a clockwise circle that is very small. Repeat 8 times then do the same in an anti-clockwise direction.

The bridge

Just the word "bridge" conjures up images of something that is strong and firm (unlike tummy of many cyclists). This exercise works the lower back, which is often a source of pain, and also the hip flexors, which can be stiff. The glutes also get a work out here.

To set up this exercise, start by lying on your back, with your heels near to your bottom. Put your arms by your side.

Without any jerking or sudden movement, gradually lift your abdomen off the floor so that you have a line from your shoulders to your knees. You will not be able to keep this posture for very

longer – a couple of seconds at most. When you
have done this once, lower yourself very gently
and repeat 8 times the first time you do it,
gradually working yourself up to 16 repetitions.

Hip extensions

The point of this exercise is not so much to build
core strength, but to build up the strength in your
glutes so that you can be more efficient in zones 3
and 4 of the pedal stroke.

This can be done lying on your front on a mat, or
with your pelvis on a stability ball with your hands
supporting your upper body by resting on the floor.
Your legs should be straight behind you, but
without pointing your legs.

Raise both legs off the floor, for a distance that is
about as high as a matchbox. You may not be able
to keep this up for very long to begin with, but try
to do this for two seconds, for 16 repetitions. In
addition to working the glutes, this exercise works
the hamstrings and the hip flexors.

Plank

By lying on the floor, face down, your elbows
should touch the floor, with your forearms making
a triangle underneath you.

When you lift your pelvis from the floor, your
upper body should be straight (i.e. do not stick
your bottom out). Aim for 30 seconds at first, and
build yourself up to 60 seconds. You may find that

the most painful part of this exercise is resting on
your toes.

Transverse plank

This is the same exercise as above, but performed
on your side. So it is slightly trickier, given that
you are resting on one elbow and your feet stacked
against each other.
The operative part of the exercise involves lifting
your hips off the ground, but keeping the body
straight. This gives the obliques a really good
workout, and helps develop your core strength.

Scissor kick

Not only does this exercise improve your
abdominal muscles, but it also strengthens the
inner thighs, and enables you to improve your
alignment as you sit in the correct position to race.
Lie on your back with your palms facing down
underneath your buttocks. Lift up your shoulders,
and then lift up your legs, scissoring over each
other. After an initial run of 20 repetitions, you
should eventually work your way up to 100.

Boat pose

This looks impossible, until you try it and realise
that it is just hard. Sit down on the floor and point
your toes out, straightening the legs. When you
have done that, lift your legs together and then
extend your arms, pointing the fingertips. Your
legs and your arms should be at a 90 degree angle.

The first time that you achieve this, be satisfied with a 5 second hold. However, you should work your way up to 20 seconds, so that you can seriously strengthen your core muscles.

As with any exercise regime, do not forget to stretch out after you have finished this set of moves. Lay on the floor with your toes stretched and your arms above your head, with your fingers pointing as far away from your body as they can. Hold this for a count of 10. Then slowly move into the foetal position, as you place your legs on one side of your body, twisting slowly to put your arms on the other side. Hold for a count of 10, then very gently swap sides.

Chapter 8 - Cycling and nutrition

When you start to take cycling seriously, you should think about food as your fuel. You can only cycle as fast as your body will allow, and even then you can only get optimum performance if you use the best fuel that you can.

But this is not the same thing as putting as much fuel as possible into your body. The quality of what you eat is just as important as the quantity. Some cyclists who are new to the sport may be devastated to find that they cycle long distances and spend hours each week on their new pursuit, only to discover that they have put on weight rather than lost it. Cycling is not a licence to eat junk food!

At the same time, cycling fast is not consistent with being on a diet – particularly given that the most popular weight loss diets of the day seem to be carb free. So if you are sad to see junk food go, you must be happy to see "diet" snacks hit the kitchen bin. Diet shakes and sweetened chemically drinks have no place in the cyclist's pantry.

A diet that is conducive to fast cycling is a healthy one that will give you lots of energy, through eating plenty of carbohydrates.

Your body burns carbs throughout the day anyway, so adding cycle rides of several kilometres a week means that you are adding a requirement for more carbohydrates. Just as a dieter is careful to choose foods he thinks will not make him fat, the cyclist should choose foods that will give him energy. One matter where the diet brigade and athletes coincide, is that there are good carbs and bad carbs. So if you have to eat plenty of carbohydrates when you are training, which carbs are good and which are bad? It is important that you understand the difference.

Carbohydrates – the good, the bad and the ugly

The worst carbs – the kind that are truly nutritionally worthless - are those that are made with refined flours. This category includes white flours, and white rice. They are so highly processed that the body does not have to "fight" much to release the energy contained. Simple sugars are just as bad, which is why cakes (being that perfect marriage between sugars and flour) are so difficult to justify in a cyclist's diet beyond the occasional treat.

Instead, the best carbohydrates to be included are complex carbs that release their energy slowly over the course of your exercise session.

While simple carbs release their energy in a short, intense spike, you may often feel a "slump" of lack of energy after consuming them. Strangely enough, some people eat these foods for the spike in energy, but forget the danger of the "slump" that inevitably follows. From a cycling perspective, a spike in energy can be helpful if you are making a sprint, but the ensuing energy slump is a disaster for endurance events.

Choosing complex carbs
What foods contain complex carbohydrates? Whole grain breads and cereals, brown or wild rice, and wholegrain pastas are all great energy foods for fast cycling. Likewise, most fruits (particularly bananas, which with their dietary fibre are the cyclist's best friend) contain plenty of complex carbs. Finally, pulses like lentils and kidney beans are great for filling you up for a fast ride and letting their energy go gradually as the race progresses.

Re-education may be necessary
If you look at carbs as a percentage of your target diet, a fast cyclist should make them around 70% of their daily intake of food. If you have been "educated" into the mind-set that carbs are the enemy, and that protein is king, you may find it difficult to re-educate yourself. However, this re-education becomes easier when you enjoy an uplift in energy, and also when you discover a drop in you're the cost of your food bills. After all, a loaf of wholegrain bread and a banana is much cheaper than a fillet steak!

The importance of protein
But speaking of protein, how much of it, and what, should you eat to become an efficient and fast cyclist. Protein should make up around 20% of

your diet. In the same way that there are good carbs and bad carbs, there are good and bad proteins.

Choosing the right sort of protein

For example, it is true that hamburgers contain plenty of protein, but that is protein of the wrong sort! Protein is important for exercise because it keeps the body strong, and to repair damage after injuries are sustained. So lean, low fat proteins should be on the menu, like chicken and fish, together with low fat dairy products. Beef can still be included in your diet, but only the low fat kinds.

Calcium, vitamins and other minerals

If protein is important for cyclists' muscles, then calcium is essential for their bones. Although cyclists are not as likely to suffer from stress fractures as runners, having high bone density propped up by calcium will help them resist stress fractures.

The importance of eating your greens

Fruit and vegetables should make up the rest of your diet in order to provide the vitamins and minerals necessary for a healthy cyclist. In particular, vitamin B6 can help with the distribution of oxygen throughout the body, which is essential for getting your muscles to work as well as possible. Bananas are a great source of vitamin B6.

Tomatoes, bananas and citrus fruits are high in vitamin C, which is great for building up tendons and arteries. But it also helps athletes to avoid the coughs and colds that can eat into your training time and impinge on your cardiovascular efficiency, so should be a part of the cyclist's diet.

When to eat

It is as important to pay attention to when you eat, as this has a bearing to when your body needs the nutrients involved.

Before you set off

Before the ride, you should eat foods that are high in carbohydrate, so that your body has taken on enough fuel. Examples could include wholemeal toast or porridge with fruit – bananas would be ideal. Do not eat in the two hours before the ride, in case the adrenalin caused by the excitement of the race disrupts the excretion of insulin necessary to start the process of breaking down the foods.

While you are cycling

You may need to refuel during the ride, depending on how long you are planning on being out cycling. A ride that will take you longer than 60 minutes will seriously deplete your oxygen reserves, meaning that you need to take on more carbohydrates during the race. You could consider an energy bar, for a swift delivery of carbohydrate.

If the ride is long or the weather is hot, consider an electrolyte replacement drink, which means that the salts in your body will be replaced.

After the ride

Now that the effort has been made, your focus should turn from getting energy to recovery and rebuilding muscle. So the switch should turn from carbohydrate to protein. After a particularly strenuous ride, you may not be able to face anything more than a milky drink. Combining milk with berries which are packed with anti-oxidants is a great substance for rebuilding the body. When you can face something more substantial, a low fat protein meal is the perfect way to wind down from your race.

Cycling super foods

Figs – these fruits are easy to eat dried when you are on the move, and provide a great burst of carbohydrate.

Beetroot – some athletes swear by beetroot and beetroot juice just before a race, while others say that it does not have any effect on them whatsoever. The science behind beetroot being a super food is that it contains high levels of dietary nitrate, which creates lots of nitric oxide. This is an important messenger in blood enabling it to carry lots of oxygen in the bloodstream. It is also high in other important minerals like sodium and potassium, so even if you are not keen on the taste it could be worth necking some back to try to get the benefits!

Bananas – being high in energy and complex carbohydrates, they are also super foods for cyclists, as they give them a boost before a race, and help to restore energy afterwards. They are also convenient to carry in a sports bag, as they come in their own wrapper.

Keeping yourself hydrated

Everyone knows that it is important to keep your fluid levels up during exercise, but how much is enough? Typically, you should drink at least 250 ml of fluid before the race, and then 100ml of water or electrolyte drink at 30 minute intervals. It can be easy in the heat of the moment to forget to take enough liquid on board as you get sucked into the race. However, if you do end up dehydrated, it will significantly impact on your performance so it is worth while trying to get adequate water into your body.

Chapter 9 - Cycling and your motivation – could this make you cycle faster?

Your cycling speed is not something that can be improved by simply reading about it - you have to get on your bike and put the hours in to achieve any real improvement. So how can you find the motivation you need to become a better athlete on days and weeks when you really do not want to know about cycling?

Set your goals

Think about it. You have goals in every other part of your life whether they are career, financial, personal, sporting and even weight loss.

Why not add cycling and fitness goals to those? Whether your cycling goals relate to endurance or speed, or both, by setting yourself measurable, achievable goals you will be able to feel that you are aiming for something concrete, and will feel an undeniable sense of satisfaction when you get there.

You could set yourself the goal of cycling at 17 mph on a flat road, for at least 5 minutes. Or why not set yourself the goal of cycling 25km in one morning. Do not be put off by the fact that elite athletes cycle upwards of 200km in a day – your own achievement is great given that you could not stay on the saddle for more than half an hour six weeks before when you started cycling.

Of course, if you are a beginner and you aim eventually to enter very long races, you may wish to step out your goals into smaller ones along the way, to avoid the hopelessness that large goals bring. So if you are entering a 40km race, make sure that you leave yourself enough time to train up to that distance, but make sure also that you have given yourself "Milestones" to check off along the way. So as soon as you have checked off the 20km mark, congratulate yourself and start aiming for 30km.

If you are not competitive and do not think that races will ever appeal to you, why not choose a particular location that you would like to cycle to from your home? You might have considered it a car journey, but before long the next town to your home town could be a swift cycle ride away from you.

Consider cross training

We have already discussed above how cross training can be a way of boosting your endurance. But different types of training can also increase or boost your motivation.

If injury or time prevents you from getting out on your bike, the gym or the pool is not second best. In fact, given that swimming uses the whole body and does not involve bearing your whole body weight, it could be first choice for people who are recuperating from an injury.

Cross training can also provide variety when you are getting sick and tired of cycling, and keeps you interested in exercise generally, which can be handy when your natural response to training fatigue is not to exercise at all. After a number of weeks of taking a break from training, your sofa can acquire a certain magnetism which can be difficult to resist. Cross training keeps you away from the dreaded magnetic sofa.

Also, the gym can also help you build up core strength, which as mentioned above is something that cyclists fail to develop at their peril.

Other people and training

Your attitude to using others in your cycling training regime will depend on your personality, and the availability of suitable training partners. If you find that others are helpful in boosting your confidence and sparring against in terms of providing a healthy level of rivalry, then getting some training partners is a great idea. They can inspire and motivate you in many ways that you cannot do yourself.

One of the most helpful ways that a training partner can motivate you is that by simply committing to them that you will turn up at a certain time, you may be more likely to turn up and not cancel than if you were planning to go out by yourself.

But if you find it too difficult to keep up with others in your cycling group, or if the criticism they offer is less than constructive, it may be better to ride out alone.

As set out above, a training partner who is an experienced cyclist may be able to spot mistakes and misalignments in your technique, or if they cannot do that they can at least take some decent pictures of you so that you can see them for yourself. It is also nice to have someone to share war stories with. Also, if the training partner is at a more advanced stage in their cycling career, you can benefit from inspiring stories about how they got where they are today, and how they overcame common problems and obstacles.

Sometimes, however, your cycling buddies have different timetables of availability to you, and that you find that you simply cannot fit them in. When this happens, go out by yourself!

Hold yourself to account

There is no point setting yourself goals if you forget them immediately, and never consider whether or not you are progressing well towards them. Why not set yourself a regular appraisal, to consider whether your goals are still appropriate, or whether you need to set yourself something more challenging? The best intervals for your own cycling appraisals are generally three months. This is because a window of three months should be long enough for you to see a concerted improvement in your performance and speed, if you have made an effort in your training. If you set your appraisal window too short, you will not be able to make much progress between them and will therefore be disheartened when you consider yourself to have failed. Make your appraisal gaps too long, on the other hand, and you may even forget to do them, or may find that your training takes you on a different path that no long suits your pre-set goals.

Another popular way of holding yourself to account is to go public. By writing a blog about your cycling progress, you are not only holding yourself to account in front of your friends and training buddies, you have a frame of reference where you can reflect on your successes.

Reward yourself

Why not reward yourself with, say, that new pair of cycling gloves that you have been eyeing up for ages when you reach your chosen speed? Or why not treat yourself to a sports massage after a particularly strenuous training session. It is helpful to create a link in your mind between trying hard and positive experiences, rather than just the pain of training.

Enter events

The best thing about entering cycling events is the atmosphere. Especially where there is a mixture of abilities, the camaraderie among cyclists can provide real support for someone who is new to the sport, or for someone who does not get the time or the opportunity to take part in cycling groups very often.

Before an event those who take it seriously may be tense, but afterwards your fellow cyclists are typically happy to chew over how the race went, and to give you hints and tips. In fact, it may be more difficult to try to stop them once they get started. If you have admired someone's performance, why not ask for some advice? There is nothing more flattering.

Putting your name down for an event is for many the ultimate form of motivation, as you have no other way to test your mettle against your fellow cyclists. Events also offer the chance for you to have your time measured by equipment that has been properly calibrated, and to have your time recorded somewhere for posterity (even if the only person who will take any notice will be you).

You can also get the chance to try out techniques that are meaningless on paper until you come across them in an actual race. For example, if there are only two of you who ride together in training, how can you really know what it is like to ride in a peloton or an echelon? But do be careful to pick one to join that you will be able to keep up with for a decent amount of time, and do not get too close to the leader if you are not confident about being able to keep a safe distance.

Find training time

Do you have time to take cycling training seriously? The problem, especially with endurance building exercises, is that by definition they take a while to complete.

If you have a demanding job and a full personal life, fitting in several hours of training each week is going to be a challenge. This will be particularly so if you have young children or other caring responsibilities, which cannot be shelved until later or easily delegated.

Think about what you are prepared to give up for cycling training, and explain to your partner how important it is for you. Do you waster hours in the evening in front of the television, watching repeats of stuff that you first saw years ago? If so, why not dash out while you have a chance instead of watching it yet again?

But the secret to finding cycling training time is to grab whatever you do have. You may find, for example, that your employer is only too happy to provide bike locks and showers so that you can cycle to work (as most large companies are keen to bend over backwards to prove that they are environmentally friendly and encourage their staff to be healthy). So why not cycle to work? You can save a fortune in fuel doing this, not to mention the health benefits.

If you do not have that option, make sure that you grab all other opportunities to cycle throughout the week. It is better to dash out for twenty minutes for a quick ride rather than miss a training session.

Make cycling a habit

If you integrate cycling into your weekly routine, it can be built in as a habit, which in turn means that it is less likely to fall by the wayside when your lifestyle comes under too much pressure. Aside from the increased likelihood of sticking to your routine, you can use the repeated nature of your sessions to measure your improvement.

So if you ride from A to B every Tuesday evening, it will be easy to see how much faster you become over a period of three months.

Keeping cycling a habit can also have the effect of signposting to everyone else how important your training time is, and that they should not mess with it. So if you go training religiously every Thursday evening, your partner will come to expect you to do that.

Visualise yourself cycling fast

Some people who are new to the sport believe that they think about it so much that they start dreaming about it. There is some truth in the fact that if you visualise yourself doing something, you are more likely to achieve it.

What does it feel like to achieve your target speed? How do you feel when you cycle past the signpost for the place you have been meaning to cycle to for years? How does it feel to have your photo taken under a 100km finish line banner? Seeing these things in your mind's eye can help you to believe that you are really capable of achieving them.

Talk to yourself on the ride

… but not necessarily out loud. By repeating affirmations like "I am going to finish this race" you reinforce the belief that you actually will finish the 50km challenge, and such sentences can replace thoughts that may be creeping into your mind like "I can't do this," and "I want to give up now."

Chapter 10 - How fast is your bike?

To a certain extent, no matter how good your technique is, you will never be a fast cyclist if you do not choose a bike that is capable of matching your performance. High performance bikes are not cheap, but at the same time you do not have to break the bank by buying the costliest one in the bike shop.

This section will tell you what to look for when buying a new bike, and what modifications you can make to your existing cycle to make you go faster.

How much does your bike weigh?

The theory goes that the lighter the frame is, the faster it will be. However, you also have to take into account the handling of various bikes, and whether you are able to manoeuvre a very light bike as well as you would like. Frames are made from steel, aluminium or carbon fibre. Carbon fibre framed bikes are the most expensive, because they are the lightest.

Some racing authorities typically say that bikes should be no lighter than 15 pounds in weight, although bikes that light are tough to manage. (Picking them up using just a couple of fingers on one hand is quite a good party trick in front of your non-cyclist friends). Race bikes are typically around 17 pounds in weight.

However, cycling pundits can be quite divided about the wisdom of spending too much time or money on a quest of the lightest bike out there. Rather than look for that extra couple of pounds of weight saving in the frame, cyclists should think about whether they can lose any weight themselves.

Carbon forks

Carbon forks are considerably lighter than aluminium or steel ones, but at the same time they are more likely to be damaged in an accident. However, there is also the issue of suspension. Carbon forks have the advantage of evening out a bumpy ride (even on roads, you would feel the difference), whereas metal forks would transfer the bumpiness and make your more uncomfortable.

Aerodynamic design

It is interesting to note that cyclists burn more energy by trying to overcome the drag force of air resistance than the physical activity of pushing the wheel around. As the cyclist gets faster, the drag effect increases and the cyclist has to work harder to overcome it.

The space age designs that you see in Olympic velodromes are not really appropriate for the weekend racer, unless you have thousands of pounds to burn and acres of space to store a different bike for each type of terrain you come across.

The aerodynamic success of a bike is largely due to its profile – so uncomplicated sleek designs offer the least resistance against the wind and are important if you are looking for high speed cycling. The features of high speed bikes are smooth, and cyclists have to think very hard before adding anything to them that would disrupt their sleek lines. For example, mud guards and water bottle holders are considered to be optional extras on very short rides for speed cyclists, because they disrupt the aerodynamics so much. On the other hand, if you are a mountain biker, you will be more likely to look out for a sturdy frame that is strong enough to cope with the terrain that you are going to throw at it.

Light wheels

Some sports scientists believe that any improvement in performance and speed enjoyed by a cyclist who has light wheels is down to a placebo effect. That is to say that the cyclist believes that by fitting these light wheels that she is cycling on a set-up that has been optimised for top performance, and will continue to "live up" to that belief by pushing herself extra hard to meet that standard. Perhaps that hypothetical cyclist might answer "who cares, if it makes me go faster?"! The other argument is a practical one – it must surely cost less in terms of energy to push around a light wheel compared to a heavier one. However, the difference in weights of racing wheel are so small that the differences are minor, which brings us back to the same question that was raised when we discussed frames above: if the cyclist is so keen to shed a few grams from their wheels, then surely their own weight should come under scrutiny first! Racing wheel have thin spokes and are very skinny. They may look delicate but are in fact very strong, thanks to modern engineering methods. The skinnier the wheel, the smaller its aerodynamic profile, and the lighter it will be. However, these issues have to be traded off against the lack of stability a thin wheel offers.

Not only are the spokes on racing bikes thin, but there are not many of them. In fact, racing wheel manufacturers seek to make wheels with the minimum number of spokes that are possible and safe.

True racing wheels typically have flat hubs, which also improves aerodynamic profile. The difference between flat hubs and normal ones may be only half an inch, but this is still enough of a difference for elite athletes to use flat hub wheels.

Skinny, smooth tyres

By having less surface area in touch with the ground than chubbier tyres, racing tyres provide less resistance and friction with the road surface. However, this does mean that they are less stable than regular training tyres, so make sure that you have trained with them on a couple of times before you race with them, otherwise you could be heading for an accident.

Flat bar bikes (or hybrids)

These are bikes that are a mixture between mountain and road bikes. A hybrid between the two, they have flat handlebars that enable you to cope with mixed terrain. They are not particularly fast as they are too heavy, but by changing the tyres to slicks you can improve your speed on the road. Likewise, by putting fatter, knobblier tyres on at the weekend, you can go on the more modest cross country trails with some confidence.

If you need or want to cycle over hills and roads but cannot afford two different bikes for the differing terrain, a hybrid can serve as two bikes in one.

A word about security...

If you have thought a lot about getting the fastest bike you can afford, and spent some money buying it, you need a decent lock. Fast looking bikes are desirable to thieves, and are sold on easily. Accordingly, make sure that you leave your bike in a safe area, protected under lock and key.

The security of your bike is an issue if it is insured. Make sure that you check the small print, and that you have met any conditions that the insurer has set (for example, locking the bike in a garage at night). Failure to do this could invalidate the cover.

Making your existing bike go faster

If you cannot afford a new racing bike, there are a number of things that you can do to make your existing bike go faster. Some of these steps do not even involve spending any money.

However, this section does presuppose that you are handy with a spanner! The tips that you can check to improve your bike speed include:

- Check that your tyres are at the recommended pressure. This can make a significant difference to your speed. Generally, a pressure of 100 psi is good, but if you have very high quality racing tyres you may even be able to double that. If you do not have the original packaging for your tyres to check what pressure is safe for their inflation, 120 psi should be the maximum pressure you should try.

- Take off unnecessary weight. If you have made yourself into a lean, mean cyclist, make sure that the bike is also as light as possible. Only remove your water bottle if the ride is exceptionally short, but other things can be whipped off with impunity. For instance, you do not need lights for a day ride, and can jettison mud guards and pumps safely for short distances.

- Change your wheels to aerodynamic low spoke count ones, which will make a real difference to your time. Racing wheels can be expensive, but if you swap them for regular ones during training sessions and only use your racing ones for "Sunday best", you can prolong their life.

- Clean your bike, because mechanisms that are clogged with dirt will not work very efficiently. For cleaning bike chains, make sure that you use specially designed cleaning liquids and lubricants (not water).

Chapter 11 – Other cycling gear that might help increase your speed

Cycling helmet

This is obviously an important piece of kit, so why not buy one that is as aerodynamic as possible. If you are spending many hours a week on your bike, it is worth spending a few extra pounds to shave a few minutes off your times.

One piece suit

Think speed, not fashion. A one piece can increase the aerodynamics of the profile that you present when cycling. Whoever would have guessed that all you had to do to get faster was change your clothes? If you cannot afford a one piece, then investing in some Lycra is worthwhile, because it offers such little friction compared with other materials.

Shoes

Cycling shoes can spread the weight of your foot evenly onto the pedal, which means that the strokes will be more efficient. But they are also smoother and more aerodynamic due to their closed tops and lack of bulky laces. To prolong their life, clean them following manufacturer's instructions as they can get smelly and dirty.

Use toe clips

Toe clips can give you up to thirty per cent increase in power by clipping your foot to the pedal so that you are pulling up at the same time as you are pushing down. This means that you can get a smoother power delivery, and avoid injury.

Installing a monitor

Some cyclists insist that having a monitor to track their progress spurs them on. Others believe that the monitor is really a distraction, and can be disheartening if it does not reveal the progress that you were hoping for. There is also the issue of its weight being added to the bike, and the damage it does to the bike's aerodynamics.

Get your bike serviced regularly

Not only does a regular service ensure that your bike is working as efficiently as possible, but it also is preventative maintenance. You would rather have a fault discovered in the bike mechanic's workshop than on the race trail, because breaking down can be a significant barrier to your speed.

Chapter 12 – Cycling injuries and how to avoid them

If you are committed to cycling long distances as fast as possible, then you will inevitably be putting your body under lots of strain. Even with immaculate technique, having a punishing regime means that your body will be under lots of physical stress. But there are several things that you can do to make injuries less likely to occur.

This chapter sets out what you can do to prevent common cycling injuries. It also looks at cycling injuries and how they can be treated.

Injury prevention

The fit of your bike

If your bike is not the right size or shape for your body, this can lead to muscle soreness, numbness, and injury, in addition to making cycling fast harder work for the cyclist concerned.

You should always ask for a test ride when you purchase a bike. A reputable bike shop should let you take their bikes for a test ride, and an excellent bike shop should insist that you do so! A decent test drive should be a proper ride of at least 5km to get a good feel for the bike (but a bike store may ask you to leave a deposit before you disappear with one of their very expensive bikes).

Beware of any store that tries to fit you to a bike based solely on your height. Ten people of the same height can have different sized torsos, arms and legs, all of which are factors in which type of bike you should choose.

Take a seat

Some cyclists never adjust their bike seat after the day that they cycle away from the bike shop. But something as simple as seat adjustment could be the difference between being injured and sauntering away from a race with no pain at all. If your seat is too high, you may find that you have pain under your knee, which will only get worse if you do nothing about the seat position. On the other hand if your seat is too low, you might get pain at the front of your knee.

It could be worth asking your bike mechanic to check your seat set up when you take the bike in for a service, so that they can make any adjustments you need.

Handlebars

Are your handlebars set correctly? You should find that you can bend your arms slightly whilst comfortably gripping the handlebars. If you find handlebars troublesome, you may discover that you have one arm longer than the other (even if this is not noticeable by looking at you!)

Pedal power

If the bike is right for you, are you sure that your pedals are set correctly? You may need to have them adjusted so that you are using the ball of your foot, rather than your heel to drive the pedal around. Using your heel can be a sure route to injury, in addition to being an inefficient technique that will not make you cycle very fast.

Shoes

If you can afford it, it is best to buy cycling shoes, rather than using regular training shoes to improve your cycling speed. If your shoes are too narrow, you may find that they can eventually interfere with the circulation in your feet and cause pain in the metatarsals and numbness. Likewise, even if you have the right shoes, you may need to check that you have not done them up too tightly, because that can also restrict the blood flow.

Are you using the right gear?

Using the wrong gear can mean that you are making life too difficult for yourself, and therefore putting your body under unnecessary strain and at greater risk of injury. By choosing a gear that allows you to cycle at between 70 and 100 rpm, you will be able to cycle fast, but in comfort. This could mean that you select a lower gear than you thought you needed, in order to maintain this level of rpm.

Are you strong enough?

If you are new to Pilates, you may wonder how something so gentle can improve your strength. However, after a few sessions, you can feel the difference, particularly in your core. You may find that cycling for long periods makes you ache in places that you did not even think you used, so core strength building can help you resist those pains.

Are you stretching enough?

Some cyclists express doubt about whether stretching can help their performance, and indeed many simply decide to get on their bike and cycle away instead of including a comprehensive programme of stretching in their warm up regime. There are studies that prove either case. However, one thing that is beyond doubt is that stretching to warm up muscles and joints can reduce the risk of injury, meaning that cyclists can push themselves with more confidence after a decent warm up.
If you do sustain an injury, make sure that you apply ice to the injury site before the area is rubbed down.

The importance of hydration

If you take part in sports regularly you will appreciate the importance of drinking enough water. Drinking a moderate amount of water before the ride will help because you can stave off cramping. Some cyclists remove their bottle holders during short races to improve aerodynamics. However, if the race in question is less than 10km, make sure that you carry water with you to sip at regular intervals. If you are riding for longer than an hour, choose a drink electrolytes because they will help your body to keep its fluid levels constant.

Head gear

Finally, it should go without saying that helmets are essential to prevent head injuries. In fact, reputable races will not let cyclists take part without wearing a proper helmet. Some cyclists initially moan and groan about wearing one (especially if you are returning to the saddle from the days when no one used to wear one), but the consequences of not having a helmet in a high speed race do not bear thinking about.

Cycle helmets have come on leaps and bounds in terms of appearance, so there is no excuse not to get one. Indeed, in velodrome cycling, helmets are part of a competitor's efforts to make himself aerodynamic.

Typical cycling injuries

Head injury

If you injure your head when you come off your bike, the damage could range from a slight graze to the cheek to a serious brain trauma. Fortunately, by wearing a cycling helmet, you can reduce the risk of head injury by up to 85%.

Neck pain

At first glance, it may be strange to get neck pain when you instinctively feel that your lower body is doing all of the work. Bizarrely, neck pain can be caused by tight hamstrings and muscle weaknesses that cause you to arch your back when riding. This is one of the reasons that it is worth strengthening your whole body to avoid injury, because whilst the legs may provide all of the power involved in cycling, they call upon every other muscle to play some part in making you travel as fast as possible. But hunching over handlebars that are too far away, or leaning over from a seat that is too high is also a sure fire way to cause neck pain. To combat this, check the settings of your bike, and do regular shoulder shrugs during your ride. You could also change your grip on the handlebars from time to time to avoid stiffening.

Arms and hands

Do you stretch your arms and hands? If not, you could be at risk of developing carpal tunnel syndrome, or cyclists' palsy. This is where you suffer from numbness in the hands or wrists. Ways to avoid this could include wearing cyclists gloves to alter your grip on the handlebars, stretching out your hands, and making sure that your wrists are kept higher than the handlebars throughout the ride.

You could also change positions during the ride, although interfering with your stance too much can disrupt your pace.

Lower back pain

This is all about posture. If you keep reminding yourself to keep your shoulders back throughout the ride, the rest of your posture should fall into line.

Buttock and groin pain and genitourinary issues

Not everyone's favourite topic of conversation, but for cyclists, there are issues with the prolonged sitting involved with cycling that mean that cycling can have some unpleasant side effects. For instance, saddle sores can feel like agony on a long ride, and when you sit down afterwards.

Likewise, for men in particular, there is a likelihood of pudendal neuropathy, where the cyclist feels an unwelcome tingling in the genital area that can turn into numbness. Male cyclists can suffer from cystitis, and from transient impotence. After decreasing the regularity of your training, this symptom should disappear in time.

For women, cystitis is also an issue, as are localised sores.

To solve these problems, cyclists of either gender must ensure that they are using a saddle designed for their sex. Women's saddles are broader to accommodate wider hips. Men's saddles are thinner, and padded in a different way.

Likewise, the position of your saddle must be set correctly to prevent injury.

Cyclists should wear clean cycling shorts every time they go our riding, which means that multi day rides may need more luggage than you would prefer to bring with you (especially if you are carrying them in panniers). However, it must be the case that slightly heavier panniers are preferable to sores in certain places!

Some cyclists claim that the best method of avoiding sores for both genders is waxing the hair from the affected region.

Illiotibial band friction syndrome

This condition is often referred to as "runner's knee", although it can strike any athlete whose sport involves repetitive use of the legs. The symptoms of this condition include a very painful outer knee, although given that the injury is caused by the rubbing of the "band" that links all of the parts of the leg that are used for bending and twisting, the pain is often transferred up or down. To manage this pain, you can take inflammatory drugs although if it becomes chronic medical advice must be sought.

Practical steps you can take yourself include checking your seat adjustment (which you will find as you read this section seems to be the single most thing you can do to avoid injury), but also checking that your knees and ankles are vertically aligned. If you are knock kneed, you may be sticking out as you turn the pedal around, which can result in a biomechanical problem that gets worse the more you cycle.

Patellofemoral pain syndrome
If you have this condition, you will feel pain on the inside of the knee. It can be characterised by thinning cartilage, and can feel agonizing. Like most cycling injuries, it is an overuse problem and if left untreated will get much better, so don't just wish that it would go away without doing anything about it!

In the immediate couple of hours after a ride, the inside of the knee can be treated with ice to relieve the pain. But long term, you need to consider strengthening and flexibility exercises that will enable you to move the patella and stabilise it. Building your quadriceps can take the pressure off the knee.

If the problem has become acute, then rest for a few weeks will be necessary to rehabilitate the cyclist enough to enable him or her to return to the race circuit.

Achilles tendon pain
Misalignment is a common cause of Achilles tendon sprain, which can be easily corrected once

identified. Another cause, perhaps surprisingly, can be improper footwear.

When deciding whether or not it is worth spending money on cycling shoes, you should consider that cycling shoes spread the force you apply evenly over the pedal. This means that no part of your foot will bear the strain of the downward stroke disproportionately, and that the risk of injury is therefore reduced considerably – simply by changing your footwear!

Chapter 13 - Your training regime – looking at the month as a whole

When you are training to cycle even faster, you need to organise your time well, to get the most out of your schedule.

But how much of that schedule should be speedwork, and how far should you push it? This depends on your general fitness, your experience, and how much time you have in total to devote to training to cycle faster.

As always, before starting a fitness regime, it is advisable to seek medical advice before you do so. This is because your blood pressure could be high, or you could have other risk factors without even knowing it.

Beginner

How many hours per week?

To avoid getting bored too easily, devote no more than three hours per week to cycling, when you are a beginner. This will not only reduce the risk of boredom, but also the risk of overuse injuries. If you are used to exercising for much longer than that, you could replace the "missing" time with some useful cross training.

How many rest days?

A beginner needs at least 3 rest days per week from cycling in the initial 6 weeks of his training.

This is to make sure that your body recovers well from each session.

What does progress look like?

The great thing about cycling is that you can build up your endurance fairly easily, by adding a few kilometres per week. This, more than speed, is what you will notice first by way of progress. It is only after a few weeks and a couple of speedwork sessions that you will notice a clear improvement in speed. A typical session for a beginner should always include a 5 minute warm up, around 30 minutes of solid cycling and at least 5 minutes cool down.

Intermediate

How many hours per week?

An intermediate cyclist may have plenty of other hobbies to accommodate, and may not have been as consumed by the sport as her advanced colleague. However, to get serious improvement an intermediate cyclist may devote around 6 hours per week to her sport. Of course, these things tend to even out from week to week, where some weeks are heavier and others lighter.

How many rest days?

An intermediate cyclist should rest for at least 2 whole days per week. Not all of the other training days should be hard rides. In fact it is enough for just one of the days to be a long ride, with the others being 10km or thereabouts. An intermediate cyclist should certainly be doing some cross training to strengthen her core, and if no other cardiovascular work is taking place then at least Pilates or the core strength exercises detailed above should be practised a couple of times a week.

What does progress look like?
Intermediate riders have typically gone beyond being satisfied by the thrill of riding fast for the sake of it, and may be thinking about entering some races. For the long ones, they may simply be happy to finish. However, for the shorter ones, intermediate cyclists may expect a respectable time, and to be hovering around the 16 mph mark on the flat, if not faster. An intermediate cyclist may also be interested in speed on downhill stretches, where there is an element of danger involved.

Advanced

How many hours per week?
It is impossible to try to restrict an advanced cyclist to a certain number of hours per week, particularly if they are in the run up to an event that has been long booked into the diary. Advanced cyclists can easily spend 8 or more hours per week training, plus cross and core training on top of that.

How many rest days?

Rest days are important generally, but particularly so before and after an event. An advanced cyclist should rest completely for at least two days a week. But if you cannot bear to do nothing whatsoever, then an exercise that is not weight bearing like swimming is acceptable.

What does progress look like?

At this level, this is person to the rider in question, who has gone beyond feeling pleased at being able to finish endurance events, and now wants to make his mark in them. Advanced cyclists want sustained speed over long periods of time, and are also after the skills to enable them to take their place in the peloton. Progress, for an advanced cyclist means continued development in speed and faster results in time trials.

Conclusion

If you are a new cyclist, you may not have appreciated that there was so much to the sport. Indeed, before you have ridden in a cycling road race and felt the effects of slipstream yourself, you may not have appreciated how important it is in helping cyclists perform efficiently.

But you will have seen from this book that there is much more to cycling fast than slipstream. Your own posture, strength and training regime all play a part – not to mention what and when you eat. The equipment involved may be expensive, especially when compared with the few pounds you have to part with for a decent pair of running shoes. However, there is nothing that can match the feeling of flying along the road at great velocity, powered by your own legs.

When you come to focus on cycling at speed, there are a few things that have to be relearned. Not least, these include the alignment of your knees, toes and hips when you are riding, but also how many times you turn the wheel in the space of a minute.

You may notice that there is one piece of advice that has not been given here: that cyclists should have to shave their legs in order to go fast. On one hand, if you consider the amount of money you spend on buying aerodynamic kit, shaving your legs must make a difference. If people are buying wheels on the basis that the hubs are a few millimetres flatter, shaving the hair off our legs is bound to make a difference. But there is also the issue of smooth skin recovering more easily from grazes than hairy skins.

On the other hand, some men do not feel comfortable shaving their legs. However, on the basis that your hair will always grow back, why not try it and see how you go?

"Life is like riding a bicycle. To keep your balance you must keep moving." Albert Einstein

Printed in Great Britain
by Amazon.co.uk, Ltd.,
Marston Gate.